June '1

Chris Earle: Two Plays

for Anna + Andrew,
our New York City
producers,
with love and thanks!
Chris + Shari

Chris Earle: Two Plays

DEMOCRATS ABROAD
RADIO :30

Chris Earle: Two Plays
first published 2007 by
Scirocco Drama
An imprint of J. Gordon Shillingford Publishing Inc.
© 2007 Chris Earle

Scirocco Drama Editor: Glenda MacFarlane
Cover design by Terry Gallagher/Doowah Design Inc.
Author photo by Mark Staunton
Printed and bound in Canada

We acknowledge the financial support of the Manitoba Arts Council, The Canada
Council for the Arts and the Government of Canada through the Book Publishing
Industry Development Program (BPIDP) for our publishing program.

Production inquiries should be addressed to:
Playwrights Guild of Canada
54 Wolseley Street, 2nd Floor
Toronto, ON M5T 1A5
Phone 416-703-0201, FAX 416-703-0059
info@playwrightsguild.ca

Library and Archives Canada Cataloguing in Publication

Earle, Chris, 1963-
    Chris Earle: two plays.

Contents: Democrats abroad – Radio :30.
ISBN 978-1-897289-16-7

    I. Title. II. Title: Two plays. III. Title: Democrats abroad.
IV. Title: Radio: 30.

PS8609.A75C75 2007   C812'.6   C2007-901293-0

J. Gordon Shillingford Publishing
P.O. Box 86, RPO Corydon Avenue, Winnipeg, MB Canada R3M 3S3

Acknowledgements

Special thanks to the following who have shared their talents so generously with the night kitchen since the very beginning: Kate Hollett, John Scully, Robert Smith, and Jennifer Stobart.

And for their crucial contributions and support: Tony Adams, Pat Adams, Leslie Ashton, Anna Castillo,* Andrew Foley, Caroline Gillis, Michael Healey, Barb Hefler, Michael Hollett, Alice Klein, Andy McKim, Ottilie Pellett, Janice Rae, Brian Smith, Crow Street Films, *NOW Magazine*, Tarragon Theatre, The Toronto Fringe, Summerworks, The New York International Fringe, and The Second City Training Centre.

And thanks to my family: my parents Richard Earle and Donnie Bundy, and my siblings Caroline Earle, Clinton Earle, and Ward Earle, for their love and encouragement; to my kids Sam and Lucy, for their patience; and to my director, wife and partner, Shari Hollett, for everything.

* AAAH! CASTELO

SORRY!

C.E.

Table of Contents

Chris Earle

Chris Earle's other plays include *Russell Hill*, *The Proceedings* and the twin comedies *Expectation* and *Big Head Goes to Bed*, both co-written with long-time collabrator Shari Hollett. He is the co-Artistic Director of the night kitchen, a company they founded in 1992. *Radio :30* received a Dora Mavor Moore Award for Outstanding New Play, a Floyd S. Chalmers Award, and a Canadian Comedy Award. The play toured to the HBO Comedy Festival in Aspen, The New York Fringe, and was adapted for CBC television. *Democrats Abroad* toured to the New York Fringe, where it won a Fringe Excellence Award for Outstanding Solo Show. Also an actor and director, Earle is a graduate of the theatre program at Montreal's Dawson College. He lives in Toronto with Hollett and their two children, Sam and Lucy.

Introduction

Conscience is very inconvenient. It's loud and almost by definition bossy. Fortunately, natural selection is phasing conscience out, and fewer of us are born with one. And the ones most of us get are withered, dry, vestigial: easily ignored.

It's conscience that plagues these plays. It's also the presence of conscience that makes them successful. From a purely technical standpoint, one-person plays shouldn't work at all. If the essence of drama is contention, struggle and surprise, then one guy standing up and talking isn't going to get it done. But in these plays, conscience is the other character, prodding the talker, bashing him sometimes, creating all the dramatic tension you can handle. And it's because the drama is so persistently evident that you can appreciate the other qualities: the questions raised about politics (some public, mostly personal); the relentless humour: the long, howling request for hope.

Chris Earle, in these plays that work like Swiss watches that explode from time to time, makes a compelling argument for the return of conscience. Bring it back, he says; if you've got one, allow it to blossom. The result might not always be pleasant, but it will humanize you, return you to the species.

Michael Healey

DEMOCRATS ABROAD

an alternate history in one act

*For my mother, Helen "Donnie" Bundy,
my favourite Democrat Abroad.*

Production History

Democrats Abroad premiered in Toronto at the Theatre Passe Muraille Backspace on August 4, 2005. It was produced by the night kitchen as part of the Summerworks Festival and featured the following cast and crew:

GREG .... Chris Earle

Directed and Dramaturged by Shari Hollett
Lighting by Mickey Wagg
Stage Manager: Amy Levett
Sound Engineer: Richard Feren
Technicians: Ryan MacDougal, Shawna Dempsey
Summerworks Producers: Keira Loughran, Kimahli Powell

The night kitchen remounted *Democrats Abroad* in January, 2006, at the Factory Theatre Studio, Toronto, with the same creative team. Aaron Kelly was the technician. Mark Staunton created the pre-show video montage.

A note on staging: in the Toronto production the only set was a chair. Sound and lights were used to evoke different locations.

GREG stands in a pool of light.

GREG: "We're a nation of optimists," she said to me once. In the room near High Park.

"In spite of everything…" And then she reached out with one of those slender hands and pulled me closer.

"You're not an optimist, are you, Congressman?"

It was her nickname for me. Because she said I looked like one.

"One of those tall, fresh-faced, really badly dressed congressmen like you see on C-Span. Sort of like Jimmy Stewart, but not as good looking."

Then she smiled, and something turned over in the dank cellblock of my heart.

Is there anything more pathetic than a pessimist in love?

It was sort of like the Film Festival, except nobody went home.

Suddenly, they were everywhere: walking our streets, eating in our restaurants, chattering into their cellphones. It was almost like the good old days—when the city was always full of Americans. Before 9/11, and the War, and SARS, and the other War, and the War after that, and everything…after. But these Americans weren't up for a weekend from Rochester to see a musical and do a little shopping. These Americans were different: tentative, skittish, less confident than what we were used to. And most of them weren't staying in hotels.

These Americans were looking for apartments.

It started out in November as just a trickle: disaffected Democrats stunned by their third election loss in a row; same-sex couples resigned to the fact that the pendulum had swung so far to the right it was stuck there permanently; war resisters—veterans of two Middle East campaigns who didn't feel like going back for a third—slipping over the border at Windsor, and Cornwall and Rouse's Point.

Then after the inauguration things started to get a little…crazy.

As usual the new guy was even worse than the old guy.

To be honest, I tried not to pay too much attention. Cuz if I did I'd just get overwhelmed with despair and then I'd lose a week sitting in my apartment smoking dope, listening to Neil Young. But no matter how self-absorbed you were, you couldn't escape it. The subject lines of my daily e-mail news bulletins told the story, accompanied by the cheery notes of my Outlook Express Inbox: *(He whistles the incoming message chime.)*

"President Pledges More Troops for Syria"

  Chime.

"Washington Issues Ultimatum to Tehran"

  Chime.

 "U.S Reinstates Draft, Millions March on Capitol"

  Chime.

"26 Dead as Troops Fire on Protest"

  Chime.

"Mass Arrests Spark Deadly Riots"

Chime.

And so on…

Then Michael Moore disappeared.

In the middle of March, two weeks before the release of his new movie, the Fat Man vanished. The silence was deafening. For months he'd been everywhere: addressing rallies, doing the talk shows, lambasting the administration. And then nothing… Last seen climbing into an airport limo for a flight to LA, but the limo never got to the airport.

The rumours flew fast and furious: he'd gone underground to organize the Liberal Resistance; he was in Guantanamo; he was dead.

And that's when the trickle turned into a flood. By May there were 200,000 in the GTA alone. And they just kept coming. The "D.D.'s", as they were dubbed by the press—Displaced Democrats—and she was one of them.

I met her at one of those welcome parties everybody was throwing that spring. It was all Gord's fault. He bullied me into going—

"C'mon, Greggie-boy, we should show our support. Besides, what else are you gonna do? Sit at home moping cuz you're broke, unemployed, and it's been six months since your last failed relationship? It'll be fun! There'll be music and dancing, maybe some hot young expatriates. I memorized a whack of Noam Chomsky quotes special for the occasion:

Using the quote as a pick-up line.

'The Military Industrial Complex is a defacto

terrorist organization...' I am so getting laid tonight...

Singing.

'American Woman...stay away from me'—not! C'mon, it'll be like the old days: Greg and Gord— out on the town. You know, if it wasn't for me you'd never leave this apartment. And you know you'll end up having a good time. You always do, right? Am I right...? Alright! ... 'Coloured lights can hypnotize, sparkle someone else's eyes, now woman...I said stay away...'"

Light change. Pulsing dance music.

When we got to the club the place was packed— mostly theatre people—

"Jesus Christ, Greggie-boy, it's like my agency Christmas party in here. *(Spotting a pal in the crowd.)* Jason—my man—! "

Toronto being Toronto, we'd instinctively organized the newcomers by profession, each group welcoming their American counterparts: our Novelists welcomed their Novelists, our Quirky Independent Filmmakers welcomed their Quirky Independent Filmmakers, and so on. Only the poets dropped the ball. The Toronto poets couldn't agree on a space for their party, and by the time they did, the American poets had fled en masse to Prince Edward County.

Looking around, I saw lots of people I knew, but felt like talking to none of them. Cooper was there of course, bald head gleaming in the halogen lighting, working the room like a young Bill Clinton. Cooper felt like talking to people. Cooper always felt like talking to people. Cooper was an inexhaustible producer-director-writer-actor- blah-blah-blah who was always working on eight different projects at the same time and making the rest of us look bad. And he was headed straight for me—

"Hey Greg! Thanks so much for coming out! It is so important that we support our fellow artists!"

Then he went off to remember somebody else's name.

I went to the bar.

Trying to catch the bartender's eye.

Hello…excuse me…look—I have money—I want to buy a drink—please make eye contact…I know what I want. Please—I'm not a loser—I promise…

"You take these?"

—it was Angela, waving an American ten like it was a membership card. With a button on her chest that said 'Live Free Or Die'—

"I'll have a Sleemans."

"—and can I get a Heineken, please? Thank you…"

Pause.

"Fire or Ice?"

"Sorry?"

"Fire or Ice?"

"Oh…right. Uh…Ice. You?"

"Fire…hot stinking Fire."

"Ah. Whereabouts?"

"New York. Just got here last week"

"Cool. Welcome…"

Clink of bottles. Show of support.

"You have a place to stay?"

"Yeah. They found some of us a house on the West Side."

"End. We call it the West End, not Side."

"Right… like London."

"Sort of… How is it?"

"It's OK. It's a bit far from downtown for my taste, but the streetcar goes right by. The streetcars are great."

"Yeah they are…they are great…they almost got rid of them, you know, in the sixties, but there were all these protests."

ANGELA *chuckles.*

"What?"

"It just seems so innocent now… Protesting about public transit. "

" I can't imagine what it's like down there right now."

"Pretty fucking scary… But, it's exhilirating in a way. There's a certain clarity to it. You know who the enemy is."

"You know people who've been detained?"

"Detained? That's polite. You mean kidnapped and disappeared? Oh yeah…"

One of her best friends had been picked up as she came out of her apartment one morning. Landlord saw the whole thing. Two guys in suits got out of a car, showed her their badges, asked a couple of questions. Then she got into the car, and they all drove away. That was it.

"—and she wasn't any big radical either. She just logged onto the wrong website, signed the wrong petition. That's when I realized they're weren't messing around. Two days later I was on a bus to Niagara Falls."

"...Jesus."

"So...who are you?"

Here it was. The moment of truth. My chance to completely reinvent myself to a total stranger:

"—I'm a surgeon for Medecins Sans Frontieres"

"—I make cutting edge political documentaries."

"—I'm a scientist specializing in Global Warming."

Pause.

"—I'm an actor."

"Me too...I'm Angela"

"Greg."

"Well you seem to have a really great scene up here."

"Thanks... Yeah, there's some good stuff...and some total crap."

"Same as New York."

"Yeah. But...it's *New York*."

An awkward pause.

"We're at a table at the back, Greg. You want to join us?"

"Us" were mostly other theatre folk from New York, but there was also a student activist from the University of Chicago, and a deserter—war resister—from Kentucky who looked barely old enough to drink. He sat ramrod straight in his chair. His hair was just starting to grow out:

"Daniel Honeycutt, sir, pleased to meet you... Thank you so much for having me."

Like we'd invited him over for lunch.

"I did two tours of duty—one in Iraq, one in Syria. Came back for my Dad's funeral...when it came time to ship out again, I just didn't go. Doesn't make any damn sense what we're doing over there—we're just making 'em hate us more."

He took a sip of his Molson Canadian and his eyes flicked around the room.

"I'm staying in St. Catharines right now. You know St. Catharines?"

Angela leaned in.

"Daniel's staying with a Quaker family."

"Yes sir. And just about the nicest people you'd ever want to meet."

"So, Greg, tell us—"

It was the activist from Chicago.

"Is Ottawa going to stand up to Washington and grant us refugee status?"

" Uh—"

"—cuz frankly I'm skeptical. I mean they are Conservatives. Albeit, Canadian Conservatives—which puts them just left of the Democrats, right?"

Angela came to my rescue:

"The Foreign Affairs Minister said today they wouldn't be rushed into a decision, which sounds promising."

"Yeah, maybe—or maybe they're just stalling until the Commons goes into summer recess."

"All the polls show Canadians are against mass deportations—"

"Yeah, but it's a minority government, Angela, and with Washington threatening sanctions, the opposition is going to try and use us as a wedge issue—"

These people knew more about Canadian politics than I did.

"Whatever. Hey, Greg—is there a good deli in this town?"

"Sure...uh...there's a place in Yorkville—and there's always Shopsy's...on Front Street—"

"Shopsy's? ...I need to meet some Jews. Where are all the Jews in this town?"

"Uh...we have lots of Jewish people here."

"Where? I haven't met a single Jew. I knew I should have gone to Montreal..."

One side effect of the Yankee influx was the sudden resurgence of the Toronto/Montreal rivalry—the two cities competing to see who could attract the biggest celebrity dissidents. Montreal got an early head start when DeNiro traded Tribeca for a loft in Old Montreal, but Toronto quickly evened the score when Wallace Shawn bought a detached Victorian in Cabbagetown. And so it went—in a rapidly accelerating game of one-upmanship: Montreal got William Hurt. Toronto: Willem Dafoe; Montreal: John Cusack, Toronto: Joan; Montreal: Steve Earle, Toronto: Dixie Chicks; Montreal: Mary Louise Parker and Hilary Swank, Toronto: Mary Stuart Masterson and Hilary Duff; Montreal: Matt, Toronto: Ben, and so on.

The Paparazzi had a field day: Uma Thurman and Jon Stewart strolling in Little Italy. Amy Sedaris jogging along the Beaches Boardwalk with Janeane Garafalo. Nathan Lane lounging in front of The Second Cup on Church Street. Somebody spotted Meryl Streep and Margaret Atwood getting their hair done side by side in Rosedale...something about that seemed so right. Vancouver did OK. They picked up most of the Hollywood lefties: Streisand, Dreyfuss, Martin Sheen. Tim Robbins and Susan Sarandon were steps from Stanley Park. Redford bought a ranch in Alberta—said he might start a Sundance North.

We all got at least one Baldwin.

Others stayed behind to fight the good fight. Joyce Carol Oates went on a hunger strike. David Mamet wrote a play called "Fuck You, Mr. President", and was put under house arrest. Sean Penn punched out a cop at a march in New Jersey, but apparently that had nothing to do with politics. Jerry Seinfeld—Seinfeld surprised everybody. He showed up at a rally in Central Park, did a brilliant ten minutes riffing on the absurdity of war, then walked off the stage, hailed a cab down to Ground Zero, and chained himself to a lamp-post wearing a T-shirt that said "What's the Deal with the First Amendment?"

Back at the club, there was a squawk of feedback—and Abigail McCall, in all her radical chic glory, stepped in front of the microphone—

"Uh…hello everyone. Can you hear me at the back? *(She adjusts the microphone.)* Hello everyone, my name is Abby McCall and I just want to welcome you all here tonight. And when I say 'welcome' I mean that word in the most profound sense…of the word. Looking around this room, at those of you who have come so far and left so much behind, and those of us who have come to offer solace and solidarity, one thought just keeps running through my brain: America's loss is Canada's gain!

So please mingle—get to know one another, have some food—thank you, Equity—enjoy the music, and remember—even in the darkest times, you still need to dance!"

Applause and cheers, and the band launched into a punk cover of 'This Land is Your Land', which was enough to chase Angela and me outside for a cigarette.

"Who was that?"

"Abby? She's one of the old guard: Agit-Prop-Collective-Creationist circa 1975. But she really walks the walk. Once ran a pig for Mayor. Her stuff isn't always my cup of tea…can get a little heavy-handed."

"It's a heavy-handed time."

"Oh,yeah, don't get me wrong. I love stuff that's in your face—as long as it's smart, and doesn't take itself too seriously."

"I'd say most of the time we don't take ourselves seriously enough. God forbid we should have the courage of our convictions… If there's anything I've realized in the past six months, it's that this is not a time for subtlety. It's a time for shouting. It's a time for crying out—as loudly and as fiercely as we can. We goddamn well better take ourselves seriously. Because I'll tell you something: those people down there—the ones who scooped my friend off the street and made her disappear—those people take themselves very *very seriously*... (*Pause.*) ...Don't mean to bite your head off. I just sorta feel like a kid who's been taken in by the neighbours cuz Daddy went nuts and started chasing us around the front lawn with a kitchen knife."

"That's kind of the way it looks from here."

"It feels weird to be pitied."

"Pitied? Angela, you're from New York Fucking City. Torontonians are obsessed with New York. We pay ten bucks for a copy of the Sunday *New York Times*, so we can pretend we live there while we read it. We laugh at *New Yorker* cartoons we don't even understand. You know what the biggest boast in Canadian theatre is? 'I saw it in New York'. That's it. And now you're here, and you need us. We're in heaven."

"Alright, you're starting to creep me out."

She dropped her cigarette on the ground and stepped on it with a New York City sandal. I watched as her foot twisted back and forth, a silver chain flashing on the ankle above. Her calf—long and smooth—turning in synch in a single fluid motion that ended somewhere at the hip, underneath her light cotton skirt. She was beautiful. A beautiful...woman of colour. Although, I've always found that term frustratingly vague. Angela was no more a woman 'of colour' than the Sistine Chapel was a ceiling 'of colour'. Angela was black—her skin dark and shimmering, her eyes a warm liquid brown. I once asked her if she was descended from slaves. She looked at me so long and hard I thought she was going to hit me.

"I'm descended from an English teacher and an air force mechanic, Congressman. How about you?"

It was the last time I brought up race.

"We should go back in. The others will worry."

We did, but I lost her in the crowd.

Cooper called me a week later.

"Hey, Greg!—I'm organizing some one-day workshops with the Americans—there's no money involved, but it's a great way to show our support and also get some cross-pollination going. Now Angela Woods from NYC is doing a one-day shop on techniques of Documentary Theatre, and she suggested you to co-facilitate; said you'd done some similar stuff with youth-at-risk?

I tried not to laugh.

"Uh…that was a while ago."

"Great! How's the 16th?"

I put down the phone and counted to ten.

"The 16th is good."

"Great! I'll give you her cell—"

We met at Jet Fuel on Parliament Street. Angela had to remind me where it was. When I got there she was sitting at the back, wearing a tank top and cut-offs, sipping an Americano, looking like she'd lived here her whole life.

"Youth-at-risk?"

"Sorry—Cooper was gonna pair me up with some

Clown guy and I panicked—"

"Flattering… How are you?"

"Bored out of my skull. I am so sick of the Expat social scene. But I've been doing some volunteer work with the resisters."

"Oh, yeah—I heard you on CBC Radio—"

"Ugh…that interviewer… 'Are you finding the transition difficult?' Difficult? Honey—the money and the temperatures are weird, otherwise I could be in Pittsburgh. No offense…"

"None taken. Yeah, we're a little fixated on what sets us apart. It's very important to us that we can point to certain things, even really little things, and say—hey—that's not American that's *Canadian*. We're sort of like the girl in High School who plays the oboe—not because she likes the oboe, but because the pretty girls play the flute."

"What is it with you people and national metaphors? So far, I've heard your country compared to a mouse, a beaver, a snowball, a skinny guy at the beach, and a minivan."

"A minivan?"

"—'not sexy, but it's safe, and there's room for everyone.'"

"So we're a little self-conscious. Isn't every country?"

"Uh…no. Arrogant. Egocentric. Psychotic. Not self-conscious."

"America—Love it or Leave it…"

"…or both…"

   Pause.

"So…the workshop?"

"Oh, it's going to be really cool. It's all about using real experience to create theatre. We put them through memory games and writing exercises to uncover their stories, and then use those stories as a basis for scenes and monologues."

Normally, I would have run screaming.

"Sounds great."

The morning of the workshop. There were about thirty of us there, mostly actors—locals and DD's. And Honeycutt—

"Oh…I'm no actor or anything, sir! Just curious…"

Cooper called us all to attention.

"Good Morning! You know, if there's a silver lining to this situation it's the fact that we have an extraordinary opportunity to meet and dialogue with each other about performance and play-making. So, without further ado, I would like to introduce Angela Woods, who, along with our very own Greg Sanderson, will be leading today's workshop. Angela is a New York-based actor, writer and teacher whose specialty is documentary and social issues theatre. Please welcome…Angela Woods."

At first she seemed a little nervous. But as the morning progressed you could tell she knew what she was doing. She had that quiet confidence that all great teachers have. The exercises were deceptively simple: describe a place you liked to hide when you were a kid, describe a favourite food—

"Describe, in as much detail as you can, something you once lost. You have five minutes. Begin—"

I thought I could just watch, but Angela shoved a pen and paper at me—

"Sorry, Greg. No spectators."

Afterwards she'd have some of us read them out loud. They were good: funny, surprising. Sometimes she'd ask us questions. She was good at that too, the way she made people comfortable, the way they trusted her. She spent twenty minutes with this girl from Ohio asking her about this bracelet she'd lost when she was ten. It was fantastic. By the end of it the girl was crying. But somehow it didn't seem creepy or weird.

In the afternoon, even Honeycutt got up. He'd been hanging back. The couple of times she'd asked him to read, he just grinned and shook his head.

"No, it's dumb, Angela…it's stupid…"

So instead, she just started talking to him. Asking him questions about the army—what he'd liked about it, what he hadn't liked. All of a sudden you couldn't shut him up. It was just spilling out of him—like he'd never talked about it before, and maybe he hadn't—talking about the fear and the boredom and the petty regulations, the idiosyncrasies of the men and women he'd served with. Watching him, you could see that part of him missed it—no matter how bad it had been. And then suddenly he shut down. One minute he's laughing his ass off—imitating his old CO —and the next he's gone all quiet, and Angela can see something's wrong.

"What is it, Daniel? "

HONEYCUTT shakes his head.

"Did something happen to him?"

HONEYCUTT shakes his head.

"You want to tell us about it? You can tell us about it. It's safe…"

And she reached out and put a hand on his shoulder, and Honeycutt started to talk.

"There was this Iraqi guy who used to deliver supplies to the mess every morning, vegetables and fruit—local stuff—in this little broken down pick-up truck. So one morning this guy was scheduled for a 7:30 delivery and he doesn't show up. No radio call. Nothing. So by 0900, we've written him off and the CO says that if he radios in we should just tell him to come back tomorrow. So then around 10, the radio goes, and it's this voice we don't recognize saying he's coming to do the delivery. So we ask for an ID, and this voice says the guy's sick and he's the guy's nephew and the truck'll be there in five minutes. So I get on the radio and I say, 'No, no, no. No delivery! Tomorrow! Boukra…Boukra!'. But nothin' comes back. And then about ten minutes later we see the truck coming down the road, kickin' up dust, and the CO says to wave him off. So we do. But the truck keeps comin'. So the CO gets on the loudspeaker and he's yelling at him to stop the truck, and then finally—maybe one hundred yards away—the truck stops. And we're all wavin' at him to turn around, and then this kid—maybe sixteen, seventeen—gets out of the truck. And he's got his arms in the air and he's yelling something we can't understand, and now the CO is getting really pissed at him and he's screaming at him to 'Get BACK in the TRUCK!' But the kid starts to unload the truck.

So now the CO's had it, and he steps right out there and he points his gun at this kid, and the kid has this box in his arms so the kid starts to put down the box, and the CO is screaming at him to freeze and the kid reaches into the box and he pulls out this dead animal. It's like a baby goat or a lamb or somethin'. And now everybody's freaking out—we got three 50 Cals pointed at this kid—and the kid starts to walk towards the CO with this goat in his arms...and the CO's got his gun on the kid, screamin' at him to "—DROP THE FUCKIN' GOAT!" and then the kid takes a step and just heaves this thing at the CO. And the machine guns start to fire and we start to fire and the goat explodes... There's a flash and a whump and a big cloud of smoke and sand and the machine guns are ripping the shit out of this kid and there's blood and fur and guts all over the place and the Sarge is down and I run towards him. He's flat on his back and I run towards him. I can see he's hit and I run towards him but I'm not getting any closer, and it's like some weird dream like I'm running in slow motion and my body has no weight like I'm in zero gravity so I can't get any traction with my feet, and I'm just sort of floating like a bubble towards the Sarge and I'm not getting any closer and I know I'm never gonna get there...

Or that's what it felt like, anyway. 'Course, I did get there... but he was dead."

When the workshop was over, Angela started pacing back and forth in front of me.

"It's totally do-able. We keep it really simple. Just let the words speak for themselves. Let *them* speak for themselves."

The room was stifling by now. Her face was shining—

"We get a small group together—five or six resisters—and we take them through the process: two or three weeks—talking, remembering, writing it down. And we just do it. Really simple: bare bones, direct address, read their stories, talk about their experiences—documentary style. No acting. Just reading. We'll do it in a bar or a cabaret—book it for a single night—Cooper would help us right? I've done stuff like this before in New York—it could be really powerful. It could be really great! What do you think? ...What?"

"Doesn't it kind of cross a line?"

"What line?"

"Between theatre and psychotherapy?"

"This isn't psychotherapy."

"Well maybe it should be. Maybe that's what these guys need—"

"No, no, no! What they need is to be listened to; to find a way to use what's happened to them in a constructive way. There's nothing's wrong with Honeycutt. There's something wrong with the people who did this to him. Who sent him over there in the first place. Look, if you're uncomfortable with it that's fine—but if you're feeling overwhelmed and powerless—well, fuck, here's something you can do! And I think it would be really powerful and really useful, and I want you to help me. OK?"

"...OK."

"OK... God, I'm melting...and starving. Let's get something to eat."

Over dinner, she kept talking: ideas about the show, news from home, politics, the war, back to the show. In between little bits of autobiography slipped out. Air Force brat childhood bouncing around from base to base: Pittsburgh, San Diego,

Tucson. A B.A. from Sarah Lawrence, Masters from NYU. A decade slogging in the trenches Off Off Off Broadway.

As she talked, I watched as her hands danced around the table: rearranging the salt and pepper shakers, refolding a napkin, fiddling with the silver bracelet on her wrist…

And then I realize that she's stopped talking—

"…I hate this…I want to go home…I miss my apartment…I miss my books…I miss my stupid coffee cups…I want to go home…"

And I want to reach out and take one of those dancing hands in mine, and say, 'It's OK, Angela…you'll be able to go home soon…"

But I can't promise that.

Or I could have said—

"It's OK, Angela…you're homesick now, but you'll get over it. And eventually you'll get used to living here. You'll learn the words to 'O Canada' and learn to like hockey and Tim Hortons…and you'll learn to get excited about universal health care and silver medals at the Olympics, and it'll be home. I promise…

It's what happened to me."

Pause.

Why didn't I tell her?—That first night at the party? It would have been so simple:

"Hey Angela, guess what?—I've lived here a long time, but I was actually born in Syracuse, New York."

But I didn't. I think part of me thought it would

make me less exotic in her eyes. Less interesting. I wanted to be her new Canadian friend. And I was used to keeping the information to myself—we usually did, we American Emigrants. The Invisible Diaspora. You never knew when it might provoke some subtle resentment. Or bog you down in a political discussion you didn't feel like having. So most of the time, we kept it to ourselves. And it was so easy to pass. A difference that made no difference.

Or maybe I just liked having a secret.

Outside the sun had set, but it wasn't any cooler. We walked east on Queen Street for awhile, not saying much. Then up University, past the fountains and the war memorials, and the U.S. Consulate, with its brand new guardhouse and concrete security wall looming in the darkness. I could see a stain on the sidewalk where somebody had thrown some fake blood the week before. Making a statement. Angela stopped and looked up at the Stars and Stripes waving gently in the floodlights. I knew exactly what she was thinking.

There are some things you don't forget, no matter how long you've been away.

"It's still yours, Angela. No matter how much they wrap themselves in it. It's still yours…"

"Fuck it… Who needs it?"

> ANGELA turns to GREG, and they embrace. Lights fade to a dim tableau. We hear a streetcar rumble in the distance.

It's funny how certain times in your life expand in retrospect. In my mind that summer goes on forever, a few weeks that lasted years. So much happening—at home and abroad, intertwined in my mind with Angela: the sound of her voice, the smell of her hair and skin, the way she moved her hands, the way she looked from a distance walking towards me.

During the day we listened as the resisters told their stories...about people we'd never met and places we'd never go...people and places they couldn't forget; seconds and minutes expanding into hours and days and lifetimes in their minds. Angela and I helped them get it all down: The order of events, the details...helping them find the words to describe the things they'd seen and done.

At night we went back to the room near High Park and tried to erase it all. Hiding out inside each other's bodies, while the air conditioner hummed and the streetcars rumbled past below. In bed, Angela was absolutely...terrifying. As if the fate of the free world hung in the balance. As if every touch, every breath, meant the difference between life and death.

It was fantastic. But she demanded no less from me. No daydreaming allowed. If she felt me wander from the moment she let me know—

"—Ow! What the fuck was that?"

"Stay with me, Congressman."

"I am."

"No, you aren't. Stay *with* me..."

    Pause.

By August, the honeymoon was over. The city's enthusiasm for its out of town guests had worn thin. For one thing, they just kept coming. Conservative estimates put the total number at three-quarters of a million and every day there were more. Ottawa did its best to stem the tide, but still they found a way through—by car and bus and boat. On foot. Some were more inventive than others. My favourite was the group from Michigan that chartered a bus for one of those Toronto Weekend Getaway packages. They arrived clutching cameras, and overnight bags, piled into Gretzky's Warehouse for dinner, caught the first act of the *Harry Potter* musical at the Pantages, and then at intermission they just slipped away into the night...

Washington was not amused. They tightened border security, instituting exit visa requirements. The American ambassador called upon Ottawa to "send a clear message that these deserters and radicals—who seek to destabilize relations between our two great nations—will not be granted a haven."

But with public opinion polls split and a minority government teetering on the brink—Ottawa did the Canadian thing and stalled for time: "Of course, we share our southern neighbours serious concerns, and rest assured the security of our borders will be strengthened with an additional 200 million dollars—blah blah blah..."

But I had a bad feeling.

If Angela was worried she didn't show it. She put all her energy into the show.

Cooper jumped on board right away.

"Guys, this is a fantastic idea! Anything you need, anything I can do—tell me—it's yours."

Inboxes filled across the city.

Whistles the Outlook Express chime.

There was a surprising amount of laughter in the

rehearsal room. Some of it nervous, breaking the tension. Some of it full-on hysterical gut-laughs—the resisters were having fun. Working together they'd rediscovered the camaraderie they'd lost when they'd taken off their uniforms and fled north. They were a unit again. Except for Honeycutt.

At lunch the other soldiers would sit in a clump at one end of the room, razzing each other, gossiping, comparing notes on their lawyers. Honeycutt ate his sandwich alone, or sometimes he'd tag along with me and Angela if we went to grab something on Queen Street. Puppydogging along on our heels, making shy chit-chat about the weather or the city. Mostly to Angela. Using her name a lot, as if it gave him intense pleasure just to say it—the sound of her in his mouth.

"It's a hot one today, Angela."

"Where are we goin' today, Angela?"

"What do you think I should have, Angela?"

So he had a crush on her. Who didn't?

It was during a lunchtime production meeting in the last week of rehearsal, that Cooper pushed a piece of paper across the table at me.

"Hey, Greg—CBC wants to do a phoner with you. Now—you were born in the States, right?"

"Uh huh."

I felt Angela look up

"Thought so. Yeah, they just want to get your take on the whole situation—find out what it's like for an American who's lived here a long time to be working with all these Johnny-Come-Latelys. You cool with that?"

"Sure"

"OK. Good stuff, guys! We've obviously caught people's attention. Call me if there are any problems, otherwise, I'll see you tomorrow!"

Pause.

"I'm gonna go grab a sandwich, you want anything?"

"No thank you."

At the end of the day, I waited till everyone else had left. Honeycutt was the last to go, drifting reluctantly out the door, watching me over his shoulder.

"Look, Angela, I'm sorry. I should have told you… I don't know why I didn't. It didn't seem that important. I mean, I was born there, but my family moved here when I was 10…Angela…?"

"I don't care, Congressman. I don't care if you were born on the planet Jupiter… What I care about is that you kept something from me, and maybe it didn't seem that important to you, but it might have been important to me."

" I know. I'm sorry. I just didn't…think of it. I don't really consider myself American anymore."

"How convenient for you. You can enjoy the show from a safe distance."

"What?"

"—Oh believe me, I wish I was one of you—all cozy in my happy little minivan of a country—all nice and safe and clean. And I could just sit back and shake my head at all the stupid flag-waving Americans, with their wars and their guns and all their high-minded talk about Freedom and

Democracy, which as we all know now is total bullshit…oh—we knew it. We knew it all along!"

"We took you in…we protected you…"

"Protected?— I don't know, Congressman—the jury's still out on that one, but yes, you took us in…and you were so *proud* of yourselves, weren't you? Like you said, you were in heaven. Plus, you got to fuck a New Yorker…"

"And you got to fuck a Canadian—"

"Well, yes…so I thought…"

"—and it was a perfect way to say 'fuck you' to your country wasn't it?"

"Oh yes, Congressman, it was a political act. I was making a *statement*…how very clever of you to figure that out—"

"Fuck off—"

"—and for your information, Congressman, I happen to love my country, whatever its sins and tragedies. It is a great country, maybe the greatest country on Earth. And whatever you think you are—Ex-American or New Canadian, you and I and all of us have a stake in its future!

Pause.

Here are the changes to the running order. I'll see you tomorrow…"

Pause.

And there you have it. The thing that sets them apart—sets *us* apart—from every other people on earth. That sense of destiny. That fervent belief in the future. Optimism. And whatever her country had done to her—enslaved her ancestors, terrorized her friends, sent her into exile—she still loved it, she'd still fight for it, she was still...optimistic. And at that moment I realized how stupid I'd been—to ever think that she'd stay.

For me.

When I got home that night Gord pounced on me, triumphant.

"Well well well! Who do we have hear? If it isn't—wait a sec...it's coming to me...Greg? Gregory Sanderson?! As I live and breathe. Where have you been, man?... Wait a minute. I know... Somebody's been doing the Mommy and Daddy Dance! *(Singing.)* 'When you're lovers in a dangerous time—'"

"Fuck off—"

"Greggie boy—lighten up! I'm happy for ya! 'Gather ye rosebuds while ye may' is what I always say. Besides, from what I hear you might not have much time left... What—you haven't heard? Big announcement coming from *Warshington* tomorrow. Sources say they're gonna lower the boom: 'Straighten up and fly right, Canada, or it's the Marines up Yonge Street with M16s and candy for the kids.' CBC's gonna carry it live. Must-see TV!"

The next morning we tried to rehearse but everybody was so tense and fucked-up they could barely speak. Angela tried to keep going but even she finally gave up: "Obviously, we all have other things on our minds right now. So lets just take a break until after this announcement or threat or whatever the fuck it is, and then we'll see where we stand."

We walked over to the Wheat Sheaf and watched it all on the giant screen with surroundsound: I was crammed into a booth next to Angela. Honeycutt was next to her, sipping a beer, looking scared. Under the table my hand found Angela's and I gave it a squeeze, but she pulled it away, not looking at me.

A chorus of boos welcomed the Secretary for Homeland Security to the microphone—

"Good afternoon. Over the course of the last several months, the American people have watched with growing dismay as our neighbours to the north have offered haven to those who would desert their posts in our armed forces, and abandon their patriotic duty to these United States."

A low hiss ran around the room—

"As they fled illegally into Canada, these deserters have been joined in growing numbers by another more dangerous group: radical subversives and terrorist sympathizers whose sworn aim is the overthrow of the United States Government—"

People were yelling at the screen now, trying to drown out the words—

"Shut up!"

It was Angela—half out of her seat—

"—no choice but to institute the following measures: effectively immediately, all U.S. military personnel on Canadian soil who are away without leave, or who have failed to report for induction, are to be placed in the custody of the U.S. Government, pending prosecution for dereliction of duty. As well, we have identified a list of U.S. Nationals who have entered Canada under false pretenses and who we believe may pose a threat to our national security. The Canadian government and law enforcement officials are now possessed of this list, and we are asking for their full cooperation in the detention and repatriation of these individuals. FBI and Homeland Security personnel are already on the ground in Canada, providing manpower and expertise. Now, I want to make it clear that these personnel will be acting at all times under the authority of the Canadian government, and in accordance with Canadian law. I will, however say this: we believe that these cowards and terrorists pose a serious threat to our country and our way of life. The Canadian government must demonstrate that it understands the severity of this threat, and must act quickly and effectively in dealing with it. The security of all North Americans depends on it. Thank you...and God bless America."

The room was eerily quiet. The CBC cut back to Ottawa for reaction, but no one from the government was 'available for comment'. Angela was still staring at the screen, not moving. Honeycutt was slumped over, his head in his hands. I think he was crying.

A cell phone rang. Then another, and another, and another...little beeps and buzzes and snatches of songs... It was the lawyers—calling to apprise their clients of the situation...go over their options... Angela's phone rang—a snippet of Marvin Gaye's *What's Going On?*

"Angela Woods...yes I did...what?...uh huh...yes, alright...thank you..."

"What?"

"I'm on it."

"On what?"

"The list. I'm on the list."

Suddenly, out of nowhere, Cooper's on his feet—

"I want you guys to know that we are going to fight this thing tooth and nail!—on the streets, in the media, in the halls of power—the Canadian people will stand shoulder to shoulder with you !"—

—but Angela's already sliding out of the booth and Honeycutt's right behind her and so am I. Then they're out on King Street, heading east, walking fast, and I have to run to catch up—

"Angela, wait a second—don't panic, OK? Let's talk about this—"

She keeps moving, eyes forward. Honeycutt is right beside her, an arm hovering protectively around her shoulder—

"I don't think she can talk right now, sir."

"—Angela, look, I don't know what your lawyer said but Ottawa could still fight this—or at least stall for time—"

"They were already in his office, Greg! They're probably going through his files right now. He told me to disappear—just get on a bus or a train, and *disappear*—"

I've got her by the arm now, to stop her—but she's still moving—pulling me along—

"OK OK… Let me help you…let me come with you—"

"What…?"

"Let me come with you. I know people—all over the country—Quebec, up North, out West—I could take you to them…we could stay with them—it's a huge empty country, Angela, we can disappear together."

"I can't do that to you."

"Do what to me? Tear me away from my fabulous life? "

And then suddenly she stops and grabs me by the shoulders *hard*—and Honeycutt's just standing there gawking like he's watching reality TV—

"Greg—this isn't a Frank Capra movie. These people don't fuck around. They don't care about the rule of law or the subtleties of human decency. They care about power and maintaining it through force and fear—"

"Let me come with you—I can help you—I can protect you—"

And then she leans in close to me, very close, and she takes my face in those beautiful hands, and I can see Honeycutt sort of sag...and I know how much he wants this touch, as much as I want it, and then she starts to pull away and I try to keep her there—

"Please—Angela."

"No—"

"Please!"

And then wham!—something slams into my back and I go down hard, my head bouncing onto the pavement—and I hear Angela scream and I see her run off—and when I look up Honeycutt's standing there, looking angry and apologetic, all at the same time—

"You have to let her go."

I start to get up and he kicks me hard in the chest and I go down again and this time I can't catch my breath—

"I'm sorry, Greg—I'm real sorry—"

And he runs off after her. And by the time I get up, they're both gone.

When I get to Union Station, the place is crawling with uniforms and I don't see them anywhere. I'm panicking—did they get through? Were they arrested? When I try to get to the departures concourse—I'm stopped by a cop dressed in riot gear—

"Can I see your ticket and identification, sir?"

"I don't have a ticket. "

"Please step aside"

"Why?"

"Security precautions. Please step aside."

"Where are you from? You from the States? Huh? Or are you just helping out? Where are you from?—you fascist redneck son of a bitch—"

And then there's three of them on top of me pushing me down to the ground and one's got my arm twisted way up behind my back and he's yelling in my ear "You wanna resist!? You wanna resist!?" And I say no no no, no no no no no…and they pull me up and drag me away.

Sound: a metal door slamming shut.

I would describe my interrogation as Kafka-esque, but I've never read any Kafka. So let's just call it a bad dream and leave it at that. There were two of them, and to this day I don't know who they were: FBI? CSIS? One of each? The tall one did most of the talking. The short one just listened and drank coffee…

I asked for a lawyer.

"Relax Greg, this isn't a courtroom. We're just checking some facts. Let's start with the simple stuff... Where were you born?"

"The U.S.—you? "

"We ask the questions. So…U.S. citizen."

"Actually, I've renounced my U.S. citizenship"

"Oh…since when?"

"Since now."

"Uh huh. What's your status in Canada, Greg?"

"Permanent Resident."

"Not a citizen?"

"Not yet."

"Not yet …? You've lived here a long time. Don't you like Canada, Greg?"

"Yes."

"Well, it seems strange—to have lived here so long without enjoying the rights and protections of citizenship. You know you could be deported? Put on a plane. Handed over at the border... See— whatever you say you've 'renounced', you're still a U.S. citizen. Still subject to U.S. law. Or not…do you know what it means to be classified as an Enemy Combatant, Greg? It means you can be detained—without charge—for as long as the U.S. government deems fit. Indefinitely. And once you're on U.S. soil, Canada can't help you. I just want you to understand what a vulnerable position you're in…

Now…when did you first meet Angela Woods…?"

They kept me there for five days. Completely

isolated, no contact with the outside world, and every day I expected the worst. Everything I'd heard about: the shackles, the hood over the face, the needle in the arm, the drive across the border and the plane flight to where? Cuba? Afghanistan? Florida? Left to rot some place Amnesty International would never find me…

And then one morning they gave me back my clothes and pointed me down a long hallway. At the end of it was a lawyer who told me I was free to go, and standing next to him—

"Jesus Christ, Greggie-Boy, you look like shit! What did they do to you?"

"Nothing."

"Well…Cooper will be glad to hear it. He raised hell y'know—blitzed the media, hired Mr Fancy-Pants-Lawyer here—called a friend of a friend of some bigwig. Anyway, it's good to have you back, man. What a week. What a crazy fuckin' week…"

Crazy was right. The city had been in chaos. Unmarked police cars screaming through the streets. Guys with automatic weapons storming apartment buildings and rooming houses, hostels and community centres, dragging out DD's and resisters, packing them into buses and vans, and sending them down the QEW to Windsor and Niagara Falls. Ottawa claimed it was a 'limited security action', not a wholesale round-up; but it was ugly and shameful and they knew it. There were some bright spots. The ordinary people who hid DD's in their basements and attics and garages. The churches that tried to provide sanctuary. The cops who refused to go along with the raids, and were fired. And the Mayor who hired them right back again. And the two million Torontonians who poured into the streets for the single biggest protest in Canadian history. 'As if the Leafs had won the cup', somebody said.

We've all seen the footage: the sea of faces and banners and signs and flags. Margaret Atwood making her famous speech about the American snowmobile on the thawing lake… Some say it was the city's finest hour. Some even say it was the beginning of the end for the Republicans—that those images, picked up and broadcast live on CNN, finally turned the U.S. public against their own government. But I think we can only take so much of the credit. The real turning point came four weeks later: September 27th, 2009, 4 P.M. Eastern.

When Oprah Winfrey went back on the air.

Whatever you think about the most powerful woman in America, she's a cagey broad. During the worst of the crisis she put her show on hiatus, and went to ground, biding her time. Waiting to see what would happen. Then after Labour Day, she made her move—announcing the show would return with a two hour special on the "State of the Nation."

It was brilliant political theatre. The show opened with a montage of clips from the previous ten months—wounded soldiers being loaded onto stretchers, caskets covered in flags, the demonstrations, the arrests, the close-up of that little girl in Seattle as her mother was being dragged away…the montage ended with Toronto—the roundup of the DD's, the protest downtown. Then Oprah introduced a glittering parade of guests all expressing their concern over the direction the country was headed: Movie Stars and Journalists, Pundits and Soldiers, the Mothers of Soldiers…and Angela.

She looked a little thinner, but still beautiful. Oprah introduced her as "a courageous young woman whose story I want all Americans to hear." And Angela told her story, very simply, and when she got to the part about a Canadian friend she'd worked with in Toronto, Gord punched me in the arm and said—

"That's you Greggie-Boy! That's you!"

She got away. When Honeycutt went in to scout out the train station, and didn't return, she knew something was wrong. She hailed a cab north to the Allen, then hitchhiked up the 400 to Barrie. From there she caught a bus to Sudbury. Two weeks later she hooked up with a United Church peace group in Thunder Bay and they got her across the border into Minnesota. Then it was on to her mom's in Chicago, and she was finally home.

At the end of the show, Oprah looked into the camera and delivered the coup-de-grace.

"If you love this country as I do, whatever your race, your religion, your political views, I ask you to think about what you've heard and seen here today. Think about it…and ask yourself: 'Is this my America?'"

Two weeks later, Congress revoked the Emergency Measures Act. By Christmas, the President had resigned.

Pause.

I got an e-mail from her, from not too long ago. Angela—not Oprah.

She said she was doing well, writing a book; working with the ACLU to try and get Honeycutt out of Leavenworth.

"If you're ever in New York, Congressman, look me up. I'll buy you a coffee and a copy of the Sunday *New York Times*."

What Torontonian could resist? I wrote back and told her I was finally a Canadian citizen—well—a dual citizen, actually. Still hedging my bets. Just in case.

Oh...and Michael Moore did finally turn up. Turns out he'd had a total nervous breakdown—stress induced—and had spent the past year wandering through South America living with native tribes and losing about a hundred pounds. But he's back—as outspoken as ever. He was even at the Film Festival this year. Plugging his new movie. I saw him on one of those press conferences on Rogers Cable 10. A reporter asked him how he felt about the future of America.

He smiled, and said he was optimistic.

Lights fade.

RADIO :30

For Shari, with love and gratitude.

Production History

Radio :30 was produced by the night kitchen and premiered at the Toronto Fringe in July, 1999 and was remounted in October, 2000 at the Tarragon Extra Space. The cast and crew for both productions were as follows:

RON .... Chris Earle
MIKE .... Robert Smith
Directed and Dramaturged by Shari Hollett
Lighting Design: Jennifer Stobart
Sound Design: Bob Derkach
Stage Manager: Jennifer Stobart
Technician: Rick Banville

Characters

RON, the talent

MIKE, the recording engineer, whom we only hear as an amplified voice coming from the control room.

The set suggests a large, mostly empty recording studio. Stage right there is a single chair, a music stand upon which is hung a pair of headphones, and a microphone. Upstage of the chair is another music stand pushed flat. On it sits a small bottle of spring water and a pencil. As the house lights dim, we hear the sounds of the city: traffic, pedestrians, voices, car horns and sirens. The sounds increase in volume as RON enters through a large door upstage. He carries a single sheet of paper. He carefully places the paper between his teeth, turns, and pulls the door closed with both hands. Immediately the sound cuts out. RON crosses to the chair, places the sheet of paper on the upright music stand, and sits. He puts on the headphones, takes a swig of the water, and leans into the microphone.

RON:

(Reading from the paper.) "Ever have one of those days?" *(With varying emphasis.)* "Ever have one of *those* days?"... *(Tries again.)* "Ever have one of those *days*?"

(Satisfied, he makes a small mark on the script with his pencil. To the audience.) Hey...It's good...*(Back to the script.)* "Ever have one of those days? Ever wonder why?"..."*Ever* wonder why?"..."Ever wonder *why*?" *(Another pencil mark.)* "Ever have one of those days? Ever wonder *why*?"

(To audience.) You don't have to know what you want. At the beginning nobody knows what they want. We'll find out together. In the moment. It's better that way. In fact, you don't even have to know what you think. At some point you may ask yourself, "Hey, what do I think of this?" Relax. You

don't have to think anything. All you have to do is listen…and even then, if you catch your mind wandering, don't panic. You're not operating a motor vehicle. You don't have to know what you want. *(Beat.)* You're the client.

(Reading.) "Ever have one of those days? Ever wonder why? Maybe you got out of the wrong side of the bed. Maybe it's in the stars. Or maybe it's just bad karma." *(He tries other inflections.)* "Or…maybe it's *just* bad karma"…"Or maybe it's just *bad karma.*" *(Satisfied. Another pencil mark.)* And me? I'm here to please. I'll say anything you want, any way you want. I'll say it fast, or I'll say it slow. Straight ahead, or quirky. Maybe you want some attitude, or maybe you don't. I'll be anyone you want me to be, as long as it's…within my range. *(Holds up thumb and forefinger, an inch apart.)* I'll even make small talk. I'll tell jokes. I'll laugh at yours. I'll listen to your suggestions, try out your crazy ideas. I'm up for it. I'm game. And I won't stop until you're satisfied. Not until you get…what you want. *(Beat.)* I'm the talent. *(Reading.)* "Ever have one of those days? Ever wonder why?" *(Into the mic.)* How we doin', Mike?

MIKE: *(Off. When RON talks to MIKE, he looks out towards audience right, as if he can see MIKE, dimly, behind the glass.)* Pretty much set to go, sir. You got everything you need? Got a copy of the script?

RON: I do indeed. How you been, sir?

MIKE: Very well, sir. And yourself?

RON: Ah, can't complain…

MIKE: Oh, go ahead.

RON: No, no. Life's treatin' me pretty well.

MIKE: So…I'm hearin' you everywhere.

RON: Oh, well…

MIKE: That's gotta be nice.

RON: Yeah, I've been busy.

MIKE: You're hot.

RON: I'm havin' a good run.

MIKE: Very nice.

RON: Yeah… How about yourself? You been busy here?

MIKE: As always.

RON: Good, good. Stayin' out of trouble?

MIKE: Oh, you know it.

RON: Oh, sure.

            (To audience.) Mike's great… He and I have been doing this stuff for… *(Into mic.)* Mike, how long have we been doing this for?

MIKE: You and me?

RON: Yeah.

MIKE: Oh, man…feels like forever.

RON: Long time.

MIKE: Years.

RON: Yup. So Mike, who else do we have with us today?

MIKE: We've got a couple of folks from the agency in here…

RON: Great. "Hello" to them.

MIKE: *(Beat.)* They say "Hello" back.

RON: Cool.

(To audience.) The agency folks…they created the spot. It was their idea. They wrote it. It's up to me to help execute their "vision." *(Into mic.)* It's good, guys. It's cute. Cute spot.

MIKE: *(Beat.)* They say "Thanks."

RON: Cool.

MIKE: You want to give me some in the air for level, sir?

RON: I'd love to.

MIKE: Anytime.

RON: *(Clears throat. Adjusts seat. Reads.)* "Ever have one of those days? Ever wonder why? Maybe you got out of the wrong side of the bed. Maybe it's in the stars. Or maybe it's just bad karma. At Chester's, we don't care what kind of a day you're having, we'll make it all better. Great food…"

MIKE: *(Cutting in.)* That's great. How's the level in your cans?

RON: It's good.

MIKE: OK. Hang tight. I'm gonna finish loading the track and we'll do 'er.

RON: Cool.

MIKE: Stand by.

RON: *(Sits back, slips headphones off. Beat. To audience.)* It's quiet. You don't realise how much noise there is in your everyday life until you're in a room like this. It's everywhere. Cars and airplanes, birds chirping, dogs barking, people talking yelling laughing screaming, doors slamming, footsteps pounding, appliances humming, televisions blaring. *(A sudden swoop into the mic.)* "Radios." Not here. *(Whispers into mic.)* It's quiet. *(Beat.)* Nice studio. It's one of the older ones. It's big. I like the big ones. Big empty studio. Like maybe there was a big noisy party here just a few minutes ago, and I missed it. Phew! I don't like parties. I'm kinda shy. I am. This is good work for a shy person. Perfect work actually. Anonymous. Solo. Just me. In a big empty room. Quiet. Kind of dark. Kind of…cozy. Some of the newer studios have windows. Some of them have real nice views…looking out on the city. Don't like 'em. Too much of the outside world. Not as cozy. I like these ones. Quiet, dark. No world. Just me. *(Into mic.)* And the sound of my voice. *(Beat.)* Could be raining. Could be snowing. Could be riots in the streets. We wouldn't know. We're just doing a little spot. "Cute" spot. *(Headphones back on.)*

MIKE: OK, Ron, we're just about set to go.

RON: Very good. So, Mike, what sort of a read are we looking for here?

MIKE: Well, let's try one pretty straight ahead…

RON: OK.

MIKE: Warm, friendly, not too much sell…

RON: Sure.

MIKE: Maybe a tiny bit tongue-in-cheek…but just a tiny bit.

RON: Right.

MIKE: Just give us that "Ron" thing.

RON: You got it. *(To audience.)* I have a certain sound that I'm known for. A certain "thing" that I do. Warm, friendly, natural. Like I'm just talking. Talking to a friend. "Hey, how's it goin'? How are you? Hey, I heard about this thing. It's really good. I know you've already got a similar thing, but I think this thing might be better than the one you've got. It's really great. And it does some things that your thing doesn't do. Yeah, and it doesn't cost that much. It's great! You should get one. But hurry, or there might not be any left." It's the "Ron" thing. Like talking to a friend. Best friends.

(Into mic.) You're my *best* friend. *(Beat.)* I had a best friend once. *(Takes a swig of water.)* Then I slept with his wife.

> *He calmly turns back to the script. Adjusts headphones. Waits.*

MIKE: OK, Ron, we're all set. Let's run it down with the track for timing. You're in after the two beeps.

RON: Cool.

MIKE: IIere we go. This is "Chester's," 30-second radio. We're adding the voice of the announcer. This is "One of Those Days," Take One.

> *We hear two short beeps as a cue, then we hear the jingle track begin—a light upbeat jazz riff with sax and xylophone. RON reads along, and finishes perfectly in synch with the jingle.*

RON: "Ever have one of those days? Ever wonder why? Maybe you got out of the wrong side of the bed. Maybe it's in the stars. Or maybe it's just bad karma. At Chester's, we don't care what kind of a day you're having, we'll make it all better. Great food, great service, at a great price. And for the kids—check out our new Li'l Chester Combo. A delicious burger, fries, and your choice of drink, all for just 4.99. Chester's. For one of those days."

MIKE: *(After a moment.)* Ron?

RON: Yes sir?

MIKE: I have one thing to say after a take like that…and that, my friend, is you are a machine.

RON: Cool.

MIKE: Hello Mr. One-Take-Wonder. Wow. That was awesome.

RON: Oh…

MIKE: Really. We're loving it in here.

RON: Great. The tone was good?

MIKE: Tone was beautiful.

RON: Cool.

MIKE: How about we do one more for safety, and then we all go home?

RON: Sounds good to me.

MIKE: Just a sec…

RON takes a swig of water. Smiles at audience.

MIKE: OK, Ron, sir?

RON: Yes, sir.

MIKE: Just a couple of thoughts from in here…

RON: Sure.

MIKE: Try giving us something a bit more quirky on that first section.

RON: OK.

MIKE: Right down to "bad karma."

RON: *(Jotting it down in the margin of the script.)* OK. "Quirky."…You want it a little bit wry?

MIKE: Wry 's nice.

RON: OK.

MIKE: And then on the back half, try giving us just a little more smile.

RON: You got it.

MIKE: Thank you, sir.

RON: You're welcome, sir.

                (To audience.) "A little more smile." Did you know that if you smile, your voice sounds happier?

                (He smiles broadly, and speaks with tremendous warmth and enthusiasm.) It's true! It just opens your throat right up. And you just can't help but sound... happy! *(Drops it.)* You can even use it in your everyday life. Say you're on the phone, talking to your mom, and feeling kinda blue, but you don't want her to know. Just smile: *(Demonstrates.)* "I'm good! How are you?" She won't have a clue. *(Reads with a smile.)* "At Chester's, we don't care what kind of a day you're having, we'll make it all *better*."

MIKE: Stand by. *(RON gets set for a new take.)* OK, here we go...this is "One of Those Days"...Take Two.

RON: *(Reading along with the jingle.)* "Ever have one of those days? Ever wonder why? Maybe you got out of the wrong side of the bed. Maybe it's in the stars. Or maybe it's just bad karma. *(With lots of "smile.")* At Chester's, we don't care what kind of a day you're having, we'll make it all better. Great food, great service, at a great price! And for the kids— check out our new Li'l Chester Combo!"

                RON abruptly removes his headphones. The jingle cuts out. Beat. To audience, giggling.

                It's silly isn't it? But the good thing is, we all know it's silly, right? It's like a joke that we all know the punch-line to. "Li'l Chester Combo." Come on. Who are we kidding? Nobody. *(Beat.)* Still, I guess it works even so. Otherwise I wouldn't be here.

Some of them are cute though. And funny. We like the funny ones. Cuz they say it with humour. Like the one with that guy, you know…with the…and he… *(Laughing at the thought of it.)* …Oh, he's hilarious! Or the one where the lady goes to the fridge and she…you know…and it hits her on the…Oh, I love that one! Or…oh, oh, oh…the one with the puppy!… Cute!…So cute! *(Beat.)* And some of them can be quite…touching. Can't they? They tell a little story…and it really makes you… *(Moved at the thought of it.)* Come on…it does. You know it.

And some of them you just hate. *(Seething.)* Oh, I hate that one. I HATE it. It drives me CRAZY. If I hear that commercial one more time, I AM JUST GONNA…Relax. If there's one that drives you crazy, think of it this way: thirty years from now, it'll seem kind of sweet. Quaint. A charming relic from a simpler, more innocent era. Like those old cigarette ads from the fifties.

Advertising plus time equals…nostalgia.

My best friend hated them all, even the funny ones. My best friend. He was…well, he was a very interesting guy. Very bright. Very charming. Very…passionate. "Kevin." Let's call him "Kevin." Kevin was very skeptical of the Powers-That-Be: politicians, corporations, the upper middle class. What was his phrase for them? *(Searching.)* "fuckin' liars," that was it. He was a writer. We met doing a play of his. This was back when I was still an actor. Before I finished turning into what I am now. I don't remember the play at all. It was something to do with war… But we'd go out for beers afterwards, and Kevin would be holding court:

telling stories, flirting with the girls from the show…and then he'd start in on one of his rants:

(As KEVIN.) They're all fuckin' liars, Ron, all of 'em. They own everything. They control everything. Did you know that 95% of the wealth in this country is controlled by just 10% of the population? 10%! Most of us don't give a shit. We're too busy watching the fireworks display. (Still as KEVIN, as if admiring fireworks.) 'Oooh. Aaaah. Hey look, there's a homeless guy—Aaah! Ooohh!' —Globalization's turning us all into a bunch of techno-peasants— 'but look at the pretty colours!' I'm telling you, Ron, the glass isn't just half-empty. It's shattered on the cold stone floor. We best grab a jagged shard and cut our own throats. Well, one more pint for me then I'm home to the wife.

His wife was an artist. "Ann." Let's call her "Ann." Good name for an artist. She was lovely. She was, well, you know…she's that woman that sits next to you on a plane, or at the other table in a restaurant. With the eyes, and the smile, and the thing…that thing…that makes you think, "You, it should be you."… That "Ann" thing. They met at university. She got pregnant. They decided to keep the baby even though they were young and had no money. So there they were, struggling along with their writing and painting, with this sweet little four year old boy. "Charlie." Cute kid. It was tough for them though. They were very different people. Ann used to tease him about it. She'd say: (As ANN.) "After Charlie was born, I did all these big abstract canvasses filled with light and colour. Kevin wrote a play about a kid that gets hit by a car." (Beat.) They were a good couple though. Kevin and I became friends, and they just sort of adopted me. I'd go to their place for dinner. They rented this dumpy little house in the east end…dumpy, but they'd filled it with Ann's paintings, and funky stuff from second hand stores…the way people like that do. I'd be there almost every night, and we'd sit around the kitchen table talking, laughing…drinking wine. Eventually the talk would turn to politics. I wouldn't say much…mostly just listen to Kevin and shake my head. *(Beat.)* I could never get as angry as Kevin, even though I wanted to. I did. I wanted to feel that passion that he had…that anger at all the unfairness, the injustice. I could feel it with him. I could share his. But I couldn't summon it on my own… *(He tries to summon indignation for the audience, but gives up with a chuckle.)* I just didn't have it. Kevin had it. He still liked me though. They both liked me. And I helped them to like me. Easygoing, fun, a good listener. And I was good with Charlie. I'd make him laugh by doing funny voices: "Hello Charlie…I'm the tickle monster…and I'm going to tickle you!" One of the family. Sometimes at bedtime Charlie would say: *(As CHARLIE.)* "Uncle Won, aw you gonna put me to bed?" And up the stairs we'd go, with Charlie on my back so it sounded like just one person. The giant Charlie-Monster. And I'd dump him onto his bed, and read him stories and sing him songs: *(Singing softly.)* "Go to sleep, go to sleep, go to sleep little Charlie…" *(Beat.)* I once said to Kevin: "You know, having a kid…it must really put it all in perspective." He said: "No, not really. It just kinda raises the stakes." *(Beat.)*

Oh, Kevin…Always so…*(Trying to find the word.)*…honest. *(He turns back to the mic, puts on headphones, and the jingle track resumes.)* "—a delicious burger, fries, and your choice of drink, all for just 4.99. Chester's. For one of those days."

MIKE: *(Beat.)* Ron, sir?

RON: Yes, sir.

MIKE: That was beautiful.

RON: Cool.

MIKE: You're the man.

RON: Stop it.

MIKE: Stand by. Agency's just on the phone double-checking something with the script. But I'd say you're pretty much done.

RON: Great.

MIKE: You want to come out?

RON: That's OK.

MIKE: You can probably come out if you want.

RON: I'm OK.

MIKE: OK. Stand by.

RON: *(To audience.)* I'm gonna stay in here. See, if I come out, there will end up being a problem, and they'll send me back in. Happens every time. I never come out of the booth until I get final approval. Not until you are 100% satisfied.

                Oh, oh, oh, my foot's asleep *(Favouring it, gingerly trying to wake up his foot.)* Oohhh ow! I tell you, this job is killing me. And some people say this isn't work. Well let me tell you something: *(Delighted.)* It isn't! I don't mean to sound like I'm bragging or anything, but I come in here, read thirty seconds of copy, takes maybe half an hour, and that's it. I'm out of here. I'm done! And I've probably made more money than most people do in a week. Gotta love it. Which is not to say it all just fell into my lap. It didn't. I spent years trying to be an actor and not really getting anywhere, and then one day I auditioned to be the voice of a talking ketchup bottle for a TV commercial, and I got the gig. It was a nice, friendly, sincere ketchup bottle *(Into mic.)* "Hey, put some of me on your burger. Come on, you know you want to." Yeah, that was me! So then my agent started to send me out for more voice-over auditions, I got more jobs—eventually I got really busy. And now, it's all I do. Voice Guy. Giving 'em that "Ron" thing.

> *Puts headphones down on stand, gets up and gingerly tries to walk off the pins and needles in his foot.*

And I don't really miss acting. I wasn't that good at it. It's hard. It's not just your voice. You have to lie with your whole body. Your arms and legs and face and hands, even. And if you get really really good at it, you know what they call it? The truth. *(Stomps the sleepy foot against the floor.)* Aaah. That's better. Now this *(Indicating mic.)* I'm good at. And, you know, I'd rather be really good at something kinda stupid, than really lousy at something important. Wouldn't you? *(Beat.)* Which is not to say that it doesn't take some talent. It does. You gotta have the knack. A lot of very good actors, very talented actors, can't do this work. They're not smooth enough. They try too hard. They don't sound...sincere. Or they breathe too much. *(Sits at mic, puts on headphones and demonstrates.)* "Great food, great service, *(Huge breath.)* at a great price." They don't want to hear you breathe. Too distracting. I hardly breathe at all. Little shallow breaths, just barely filling the top of my lungs. *(Demonstrates.)* "Great food, great service, *(Tiny breath.)* at a great price." It's a knack.

Warm, friendly, sincere. Trust me.

MIKE: Ron?

RON: Yes, sir.

MIKE: Looks like you're not gonna get off that easy.

RON: Ah. Too good to be true.

MIKE: You know it. We've got a little script change for you.

RON: OK.

MIKE: Apparently the price should read "4.69" not "4.99."

RON: OK, "69."

MIKE: That's it.

RON: (Corrects script.) That's a better deal.

MIKE: ...Yeah. Give me three in a row wild and I'll see if I can't just drop one in.

RON: You got it. Mike, you want just the "4.69" or should I give you the "all for just" as well?

MIKE: Just a sec. (Pause.) Ron?

RON: Yes, sir.

MIKE: "All for just 4.69."

RON: OK.

MIKE: Three in a row.

                (Beat.) This is "One of Those Days," Take Three, wild lines: alternate price...and we're rolling. Anytime.

RON: "All for just 4.69." (Beat.) "All for just 4.69." (Beat. Throat clear.) "All for just 4.69."

MIKE: Can you lean on the "just" a bit for me Ron?

RON: I surely can.

MIKE: Still rolling. Three more.

RON: "All for just 4.69."

            (Beat.) "All for just 4.69." *(Beat.)* "All for *just* 4.69."

MIKE: Good. I think we have one there. Stand by.

RON: *(Beat.)* Hey Mike.

MIKE: Yeah?

RON: Listen to this. I read somewhere that people who work in advertising are artists with nothing to say.

MIKE: Oh yeah?

RON: Yeah. Which I think is pretty unfair. I mean, I got something to say.

MIKE: What's that?

RON: *(Yelling into the mic.)* "BUY THIS! BUY THIS! BUY THIS! BUY THIS!"

MIKE: *(Chuckling.)* The agency folks are killing themselves, Ron.

RON: Cool.

MIKE: Very funny. Stand by.

RON: *(Takes a swig of water, and waits. To audience.)* I saw a guy die in here once. Not physically. But I think it was the kind of mental meltdown that you never really recover from. He was an older guy. A real old-fashioned "Voice of God" type of announcer. *(Imitating the Voice of GOD.)* "ALL FOR JUST 4.69." It was the kind of voice that used to sell everything. A famous voice. You've heard it. Rich. Authoritative. Clients loved him. A total pro. Very respected. But his type has been out of fashion for quite awhile. Now it's the voice of…a friend.

RON stands, adjusts mic., and acts out the story.

So this guy and I were doing a session together...this was well after the guy's heyday, right, but he's still doin' OK. Still working. So we're doin' this thing. I'm being the quirky guy and he's coming in at the end with the big announce. Pretty straightforward: here's the product—here's the price—think how much you'll save— *(As GOD.)* "but hurry, or there might not be any left." And this young guy from the agency—he's maybe twelve years old, but already dressing like a teenager—this agency geek starts to fuck with the old guy's read:

MIKE: *(As the unseen AGENCY GEEK.)* Um, could you maybe be a little more casual, more...natural?

RON: *(As GOD.)* Gotcha.

GEEK: Like, just say it like you're talking to a friend. Not so announcer-y.

RON: *(To audience.)* Which is ludicrous, right? Because that's what this guy is. It's what he's always been. So...God tries to do the friendly, intimate, off-the-cuff thing, and it's just not working.

            (As GOD, attempting a friendly read.) "But hurry, or there might not be any left." It doesn't sound...sincere.

GEEK: Um. You know what? Go back to what you were doing...before.

RON: *(As GOD.)* Gotcha. *(To audience.)* But it's too late. He's done something to God, made him question his whole approach to the read, who knows? Maybe question his whole approach to life. And then it happens. It was just a little stumble. A little extra sound—a mouth sound—on the word "participating." "Available at participating retailers." A click or a smack or something. Tongue against teeth.

GEEK: We got a little glitch there. Let's do it again. This is "Big Savings," Take Seven.

GOD: "Available at participaking retailers..." Whoops. Sorry about that.

GEEK: This is "Big Savings," Take Eight.

GOD: "Available at partishipating..." Hmmn. I really should stop drinking at breakfast. Heh heh.

GEEK: "Big Savings," Take Nine.

RON: *(To audience.)* And I can see it happen. I can feel it. That moment. When his confidence just— whoosh—evaporates *(Into the mic.)* "the way only confidence can." *(As GOD.)* "Available at partspating..." Oh, this is silly. *(Throat clear.)* OK, here we go. Here's the one:

GEEK: Take Ten.

GOD: "Available at parstipulating..." *(Beat.)* "Availabuh..." *(Beat. GOD tries very hard.)* "Avai..."

GEEK: *(Beat.)* Um...do you want to come out for a minute? Get some water or...something? *(GOD shakes his head.)* I think maybe you should you come out...take a little break. *(GOD shakes his head again. Beat.)* ...Ron? For this next take, could you please do the announcer lines as well?

RON: *(Beat.)* Now I guess I could have said "No," but what good would that have done? They needed the lines. He couldn't do it. So I did it. With God still in the booth with me. He wouldn't come out. Just stood there, staring at his script. *(Into the mic softly, warm and friendly.)* "Available at participating retailers." *(Beat.)* And whenever the spot would come on the radio, I swear I could hear, right after the word "participating," a little, tiny… *(He gives a tiny, tiny sob into the mic. Beat. RON stares at the audience, then turns back to the mic.)* How we doing, Mike? *(Beat.)* Mike?

MIKE: Sorry for the wait, sir. I got another change for you.

RON: OK.

MIKE: The line "At Chester's, we don't care what kind of day you're having," now reads "It doesn't matter what kind of day you're having."

RON: *(Scribbling the change on his script.)* OK. So it's "At Chester's, it doesn't matter what kind of day you're having."

MIKE: That's it. There was a feeling that "we don't care" sounded a little callous.

RON: Right. Sure.

MIKE: So let's take the whole thing from the top and just give me that exact same read on "4.69."

RON: OK.

MIKE: OK, here we go. This is "One of Those Days," Take Four, and…

RON: Sorry, Mike. But which read?

MIKE: Sorry?

RON: You want the "All for *just* 4.69" read?

MIKE: Yeah. The last one you did.

RON: Where I hit the "just."

MIKE: That's it. Otherwise give me everything else exactly the same.

RON: With "It doesn't matter."

MIKE: "It doesn't matter."

RON: Gotcha.

MIKE: OK, here we go. This is "One of Those Days" ...Take Four.

RON: *(Jingle begins.)* "Ever have one of those days? Ever wonder why? Maybe you got out of the wrong side of the bed. *(The jingle track cuts out.)* Maybe it's in the stars..." *(RON looks to the booth, confused.)*

MIKE: You OK sir?

RON: Yeah. What happened?

MIKE: Um. You stopped talking.

RON: No, I lost the track in my phones.

MIKE: You did?

RON: Yeah, it cut right out.

MIKE: That's weird. We didn't lose it in here.

RON: It cut out right after "wrong side of the bed."

MIKE: You can hear me OK now?

RON: Sure.

MIKE: Don't know. Maybe some bug in the software. Stand by. I'm just going to check something out...

RON: Cool.

             (Beat. To audience.) Mike's gonna check something out. Please stand by. We are experiencing technical difficulties. *(Takes a swig of water. Hums a bit of the jingle track. Into mic.)* There's a city out there... *(Beat.)*

             I'm always thinking I'm going to run into him. On the street, at a store...Part of me is always looking for him; entering a restaurant, I'll quickly scan the faces. Kevin? No. Kevin? No. Kevin? No. Kevin? NoKevinNoKevinNoKevinNoKevinNoKevinno kevinno kevinno… Good. It's safe. *(Sits.)*

Kevin and I had been friends for about six months when he asked me to sleep with his wife. *(Beat.)* We'd been out late drinking. Kevin invited me back to their place to crash. When we got there, most of the lights were off, Ann and Charlie had already gone to bed. So…we're standing there in the front hall, a little drunk, whispering, trying not to laugh… And Kevin comes up with this idea. A crazy idea. But I'm up for it, I'm game. So…we go up the stairs together, with synchronized steps, trying to sound like one person…so Ann won't know I'm there. Then down the hall to their bedroom. The door is ajar. In the darkness I can make out the shape of Ann, asleep in bed, facing away from us towards the wall. We go in. I look at Kevin. He's nodding, grinning. I'm just about his height, his build. I start to undress. It's so hard not to laugh. Ann stirs for a moment. I hold my breath. Then I take off the rest of my clothes, creep to the bed, get in, and lie down next to my best friend's wife. My body is very close to hers, but not touching. I think she was wearing a t-shirt, or a pajama top. Something. I can hear her breathing, soft regular breaths. Then she shifts, turns towards me, in her sleep. Snuggles up to me, an arm across my chest, her knee up over my thigh, her cheek against my shoulder. *(Beat.)* And she thinks I'm *him. (As ANN.)* "Hey, sweetie, did you have a nice time?" "Uh huh." "Did you turn the porch light off?" *(Trying to stifle a laugh.)* "Uh huh."

And I can feel her trust. I can feel it in her body, the weight of it against me, her breath on my shoulder. And I start to think that maybe…this isn't a good idea. I can see Kevin in the doorway, backlit by the light from the hall, shaking with laughter. *(As ANN, sleepily snuggling up to RON.)* "Are you OK?...sweetie?...Kevin? *(RON tries to stifle his laughter.)* ...Kevin?...Kevin, say something!" Kevin slams the light on: "What in the name of God is GOING ON HERE?"... *(Giggling.)* She was...really mad. I mean, imagine: you think you know who somebody is, you're absolutely sure of it, and then—*(Finger snap.)*—they're not. They're somebody else. *(As ANN.)* "Kevin, what the FUCK do you think you're DOING?!" *(As KEVIN, drunk and laughing.)* "Oh come on...Ann, it was a JOKE...sweetie...come on...It's just Ron!" I put my clothes back on and went and slept on the couch. *(Beat.)*

Kevin could be a bit of an asshole sometimes. But then again, who isn't?

> *RON turns back to his script. Then wincing, shifting in his seat.*

Oh, oh, oh. Now my ass is asleep *(Stands up, tries to shake it off.)* Oh no. I don't think it's just asleep. I think it's in a coma. Wakey wakey. *(Slaps his ass.)* I got numb bum. Oh, oh, oh. No. no. My ass is dead... *(Into mic.)* Mike. Hey, Mike. I think my ass is dead. Call an ambulance Mike, we got a dead ass in Studio Three. Ow. Ow. Ow. Hello Mike...Yoo-hoo Mike... *(Singing.)* Ground Control to Major Mike... "Open the pod door, Hal" ..."I'm sorry, Dave, I can't do that...no Dave, don't...Daisy, Daisy, give mee your aannnssweerrr truuuueeeee..." Mike? Hello Mike. Come in, Mike. Can you hear...

MIKE: —and smooth, OK?

RON: Sorry, Mike I didn't get that.

MIKE: Didn't get what?

RON: I just caught the end of that. The talkback wasn't on or something.

MIKE: Sorry. Let's take the whole thing again. Keep it happy. Keep it smooth. And don't forget the "just 4.69."

RON: Gotcha.

MIKE: This is "One of Those Days"…Take Five…and here it comes.

RON: *(Jingle starts. RON starts laughing.)* Sorry…I'm sorry, Mike. OK. Here we go.

MIKE: *(A chuckle.)* Take Six.

RON: *(Jingle starts.)* "Ever have one of those days? Ever wonder why?" Maybe you got out of the wrong side of the bed, maybe it's in the stars, or maybe it's just bad karma. At Chester's, we don't care what kind of a day you're having, we'll make it all better. Great food—" *(Jingle track cuts out.)*

MIKE: Ron. "It doesn't matter."

RON: What?

MIKE: The line is "It doesn't matter what kind of day you're having."

RON: Whoops. Sorry about that.

MIKE: OK, here we go…Oh and you might wanna just back off the mic a bit, Ron…and keep an eye out for the breathing.

RON: *(Beat.)* Too much breathing?

MIKE: Yeah. This is "One of Those Days"…Take Seven…

RON: Where are you hearing me breathe?

MIKE: Sorry. All set?

RON: No. Mike, where are you hearing me breathe?

MIKE: Yes we are, sir…

RON: No, Mike…you said you could hear me breathe. Where was it?

MIKE: I think it was just a general thing.

RON: *(Beat.)* OK.

MIKE: This is "Days"…Take Seven.

RON: *(Jingle.)* "Ever have one of those days? Ever wonder why? Maybe you got out of the wrong side of the bed. Maybe it's in the stars. Or maybe it's just bad karma. At Chester's it"— *(Jingle stops.)*

MIKE: Sorry, Ron. It's after "karma."

RON: What?

MIKE: The breath. We're hearing you breathe after "karma."

RON: Really.

MIKE: Yeah, try not to breathe there.

RON: That'll be hard. It's kind of the logical place to breathe.

MIKE: How bout after "Combo"?

RON: That's a long ways in.

MIKE: I think you can do it.

RON: What about after "stars"?

MIKE: Just so long as we don't hear it.

RON: You won't.

MIKE: This is "Days," Take Eight…

RON: *(Jingle.)* "Ever have one of those days? Ever
                wonder why? Maybe you got out of the wrong side
                of the bed. *(Long beat.)* Maybe it's in the stars, or
                maybe"...

MIKE: Whoa, Ron, 30-second radio buddy. Big pause
                after "Bed"...

RON: Yeah, I know. You just kinda got me thinking about
                my breathing...

                (A joke.) You're freakin' me out man.

MIKE: *(Beat.)* You set, sir?

RON: Yeah.

MIKE: This is "Days," Take Nine.

RON: *(Jingle.)* "Ever have one of those days? Ever
                wonder why? OK, here we go. Keep it smooth,
                keep it warm, keep it friendly. Talking to a friend.
                Don't breathe...don't breathe...don't fail. You
                mustn't fail...you can't fail...yeah... *(With a
                "smile.")* You're going to fail. You're going to fail.
                You're going to screw it up. Come on. Screw it up.
                Screw it up now. Now. NOW! *(Jingle cuts out. Beat.)*
                Sorry.

MIKE: Got a little slur on "Chester Combo."

RON: I meant to do that.

MIKE: *(Beat.)* We're all set in here, sir.

                    *RON clears throat, adjusts headphones. Suddenly
                    realizes something.*

RON: Mike, look at me. What's wrong with this picture?

MIKE: I have no idea.

RON: I'm standing! I never stand. Right? I always sit
                down, right? Every time!

MIKE: You wanna sit down?

RON: Yeah. Of course I want to sit down. That's part of my thing. No wonder I was screwing up. *(He readjusts mic and sits.)*

MIKE: You want me to come in there, sir?

RON: No. It's fine. I got it. *(Beat.)* OK...there we go. That's better.

MIKE: *(A sudden burst of laughter as if sharing a joke with the agency folks.)* Yeah...exactly!... *(Beat.)* OK. You all set, sir?

RON: *(Beat.)* Yeah.

MIKE: OK. Just keep it smooth. This is the one...This is "Days," Take Ten...

RON: *(Jingle starts.)* "Ever have one of those days? Ever wonder why?"...now why was he laughing? Was he laughing at me? And why did he say "this is the one?" 'Cuz even if it was the one, now it's not going to be the one, 'cuz he said it was gonna be the one... OK, keep it warm, keep it smooth, keep it friendly. Talkin' to a friend. Good...good. It's going well; maybe this is the one. What's that word...? What the hell is that word? F-o-o-d. It's coming up and I have no idea how to say that word. I have no idea how my tongue and lips and teeth are gonna make that sound: Fa—Fow—Fowo—Foo—Foo FOWODUH! *(Jingle cuts out. A long beat.)* ...Sorry...

MIKE: *(Beat.)* You need a sec, sir?

RON: No.

MIKE: Stand by...

       RON adjusts headphones. Clears throat. Waits.

MIKE: *(As if to agency folks.)* Yeah I know...I know... *(To RON.)* OK. This is "Days." Take Eleven.

RON: *(Jingle track begins.)* "Ever have one of those days?
                Ever wonder why? Maybe you got out of the
                wrong side of the bed. Maybe it's in the stars. Or
                maybe those agency folks are on the phone right
                now: 'Hey, Ron's not really working out for the
                sound we're looking for. Let's get that new guy in
                here. Yeah…he's cooler, hipper.' *(As the new guy—
                younger, hipper.)* 'Great food, great service, at a
                great price.' 'Yeah! That's the guy. Let's get him in
                here. We'll just tell Ron he's done. He can come on
                out. And then we'll redo it. We'll replace him with
                the new guy!'"

                *RON rips off headphones, jingle stops. Beat. To
                audience.*

                They can replace you any time.

                (Beat.) Kevin went away. He decided to go back to
                school and finish his master's in…something. I
                can't remember what. Something…worthwhile.
                The school was out of town. He was going to spend
                the week there and then come back into town on
                the weekends to be with his family. Ann and
                Charlie. And me. 'Cuz I was one of the family.
                Except, he didn't come home every weekend.
                Every other weekend. Maybe. And I think he and
                Ann started to have some problems. It was hard.
                The separation. We'd talk on the phone: "I'm good,
                how are you?" *(As KEVIN.)* "I'm shitty, Ron…I'm
                shitty."

                I don't remember a lot from that time. Just little
                snapshots here and there…I remember having
                dinners with Ann and Charlie. Helping put Charlie
                to bed. And sitting up with Ann: talking, drinking
                wine…I remember her being lonely. And
                uncertain. "I don't know what I want." And me,
                being there for her: listening…talking…warm,
                friendly…sincere. With a smile in my voice. *Trust
                me.* …And well, you know how these things

happen: slowly, imperceptibly… Like a glass being nudged to the edge of a table… "I worry about you." Nudge.

"I care about you." Nudge.

"I should go home." Nudge.

"You don't have to." Nudge.

"Life's funny." Nudge.

"What?" Nudge.

"Just, you know…" Nudge.

"You know what?" Nudge.

"What?" Nudge.

"I think you need a hug."

(Into mic, softly.) Smash…

And I remember going up the stairs, walking together, so we sounded like one person. And down the hall. And into her bed. Their bed.

And, well, you know…

You've done it…

(Into mic., very softly.)…with the dark…and her hair…and your hands…and her hips, and your lips, and her neck, and your fear. And her courage… *(Long beat.)* And it was so…quiet. Just her breathing. And mine… *(He breathes very softly into the mic. Beat.)*

And I remember the sound of the front door opening. The sound of a man coming home. And Ann putting a hand on my shoulder: "Just stay here." And she put on a robe…and she went downstairs…and she told him.

Oh Ann…

And I remember the sound of Kevin calling my name.

(A howl of rage.) "RON!…COME ON DOWN, RON…COME ON DOWN YOU FUCKIN' LIAR!"

(Beat. To audience.) I guess I could have gone down. But what good would that have done? So I just lay there, staring at the ceiling…until he left. And after a long, long time, Ann came back up the stairs. *(Silence. He slowly turns back to the mic. He puts his headphones back on. Jingle resumes and finishes. He is very still.)*

MIKE: Ron?…Ron, sir?

RON: *(Softly.)* Yes, sir.

MIKE: Nice take.

RON: Thanks.

MIKE: Beautiful. We're very happy. You, sir, are done.

RON: Really?

MIKE: Come on out.

RON: *(Beat.)* Don't you want to do a playback, Mike?

MIKE: No. We're fine. We're happy.

RON: What about the client?

MIKE: The client's happy.

RON: *(Looking at the audience.)* I don't think so.

MIKE: The client's happy.

RON: Not a hundred percent. *(Beat.)* I think they know what they want now.

MIKE: Oh?

RON: Let me try one more. For safety.

MIKE: One more?

RON: For safety. *(Beat. Pleading.)* Mike?

MIKE: *(Beat.)* Stand by. This is "Days" Safety, Take
             Twelve…we're rolling…

RON: *(Jingle starts.)* "Ever have one of those days? Ever
             wonder why? Maybe you got out of the wrong side
             of the bed. Or the right side, of the wrong bed. Or
             maybe it's just bad karma. You knew what you
             wanted. What you thought. Who you were. Who
             you are… Who am I? I'm the talent: Great food,
             great service, at a great price. A great price! Such a
             GREAT PRICE!" *(Jingle stops.)* Shit. Popped the
             "P." OK , let's go…

MIKE: Uh…sir?

RON: Let's do it again. I know what it is…

MIKE: Uh…I really think…

RON: No, no. Let's go. Right away. Come on. I got it. This
             is the one…

MIKE: *(Beat.)* This is Thirteen.

RON: *(Jingle.)* "Ever have one of those days? Ever
             wonder why?"…They made it. Kevin and Ann.
             They're still together. They weathered the storm.
             Weathered me. They survived the "Ron" thing…
             And little Charlie… "And for the kids, check out
             our new Li'l Chester Combo!" He must be a big boy
             now. I miss them. My friends. My family…I can't
             get the smile out of my voice… Nobody is
             LISTENING TO ME!

             (Jingle is cut off.) …Sorry…

MIKE: *(Beat.)* This is Fourteen.

RON: *(Jingle.)* "Ever have one of…" *(He stops. The jingle stops.)*

MIKE: *(Beat.)* Fifteen. *(Jingle.)*

RON: *(With increasing desperation.)* "Ever hav—" *(He stops. Jingle stops.)*

MIKE: *(Beat.)* Sixteen. *(Jingle.)*

RON: "Ev—" *(He stops. Jingle stops.)*

MIKE: *(Beat.)* Seventeen. *(Jingle.)*

> *RON opens his mouth to speak but nothing comes out. He tries again and again, but each time the sound dies in his throat. The jingle stops. Lights on RON fade, mouth open, mute before the microphone. All we can hear is the sound of his breathing.*

> *Blackout.*